# Love Is Everywhere

### Wisdom from Grandma Series – Book 2

## Grace Boucaud-Moore

Illustrated by Christopher Greaves

All scripture quotations, unless otherwise indicated, are taken from the Holy Bible, King James Version. Public domain.

Scripture quotations marked ICB are taken from The Holy Bible, International Children's Bible® Copyright© 1986, 1988, 1999, 2015 by Thomas Nelson. Used by permission.

Copyright © 2023 Grace Boucaud-Moore
Copyright © 2023 TEACH Services, Inc.
ISBN-13: 978-1-4796-1573-5 (Paperback)
ISBN-13: 978-1-4796-1574-2 (ePub)
Library of Congress Control No: 2023917445

**He First Loved Me**

When God made me
He thought of everything—
All I would need to be happy,
What things would make my heart sing.

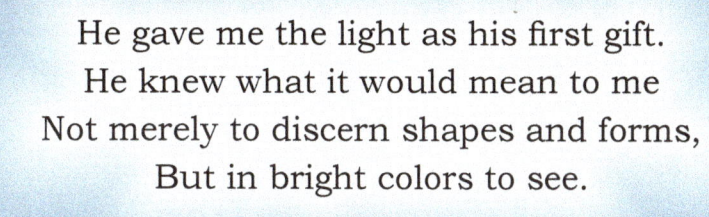

He gave me the light as his first gift.
He knew what it would mean to me
Not merely to discern shapes and forms,
But in bright colors to see.

God thought I would love sweet aromas,

And so He created the air.

He filled the earth with rich flora,

And hung fragrant flowers everywhere.

To God, these gifts were not enough

The extent of His love to declare.

He hung the sun, moon, and stars in the heavens

To amaze me with jewels so fair.

To show me that love just gets better,

God called forth all birds and fish.

Their colors, shapes, sounds, and maneuverings

Are more than any person could wish.

The animals, God gave as a bonus

To fill me with more wonder yet.

And then it was time to surprise me,

So He woke me and then our eyes met.

He greeted me with warm affirmation—

I could tell I was precious to him!

We two shared a most special kinship;

We'd be friends through the thick and the thin.

His desire is for me, forever.

He is mine, and I belong to Him.

All my joy I find in His presence,

And He truly shields me from sin.

**Genesis 3:15** "I will make you and the woman enemies to each other. Your descendants and her descendants will be enemies. Her child will crush your head. And you will bite his heel" (ICB).

**Deuteronomy 30:6** "And the Lord thy God will circumcise thine heart, and the heart of thy seed, to love the Lord thy God with all thine heart, and with all thy soul, that thou mayest live."

## Like God

I too, am a child of God,
Created in His image I am.
And as an image bearer,
I am reflective of Him.

I have a desire for relationships—
Like the One who created me.
Unlike the myriad of creatures,
I'm governed by God's morality.

The Father gives me understanding,
Another's perspective to see;
I find it's the path to accepting
Somebody other than me.

Though our personalities may differ,
We must love and accept from our hearts,
For our friendships make us richer
When we draw together, not apart.

Differences oft will cause challenge
But we can reason and speak.
With truth and God's courage to guide us
His children should never be weak.

God showed us such love in creation
'Twas a lesson, to teach us the way—
How we too can love one another
And live life in the very best way.

Always think well of others

When serving in word or in deed,

And be sure to consider their feelings

As well as to meet their needs.

Like God, we can be deeply committed

To the creatures all around;

We can choose to be his dear children,

And in his kingdom be found.

**Genesis 1:27** "So God created human beings in his image. In the image of God he created them. He created them male and female" (ICB).

## What Is Love?

Love is the revealing of God;
All agree it is a beautiful thing.
At the creation of all things good,
Love inspired God's angels to sing.

**1 John 4:7, 8** "Dear friends, we should love each other, because love comes from God. The person who loves has become God's child and knows God. Whoever does not love does not know God, because God is love" (ICB).

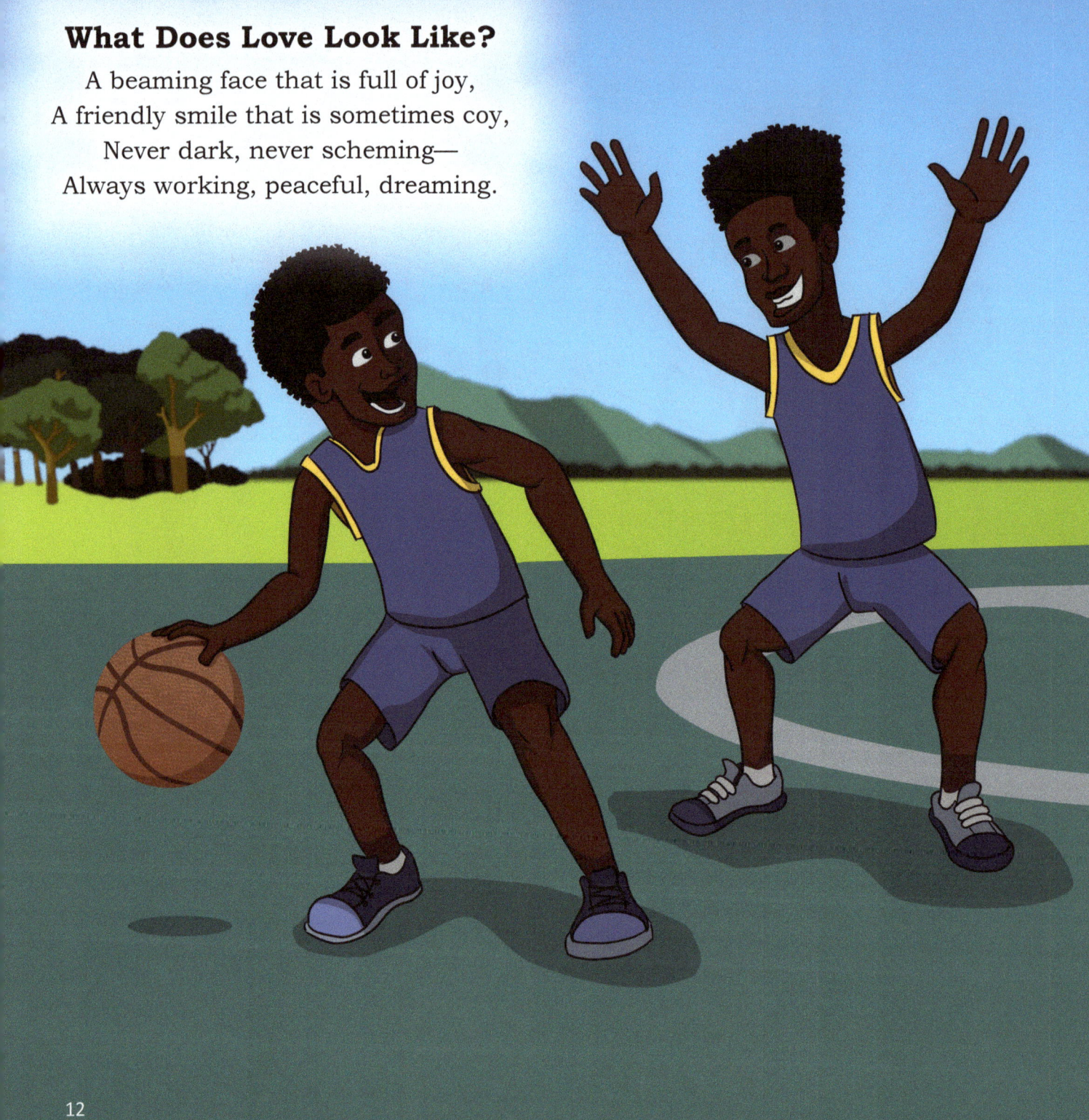

**What Does Love Look Like?**

A beaming face that is full of joy,
A friendly smile that is sometimes coy,
Never dark, never scheming—
Always working, peaceful, dreaming.

**Jeremiah 29:11** "'I say this because I know what I have planned for you,' says the Lord. 'I have good plans for you. I don't plan to hurt you. I plan to give you hope and a good future'" (ICB).

## How Does Love Feel?
Soft and cuddly like my bear,
Often playful like the air,
Warm and lovely like the sun,
Strong as the rock I'm standing on.

**Ezekiel 16:3-6** "This is what the Lord God says to Jerusalem: 'Your beginnings and your ancestors were in the land of the Canaanites. Your father was an Amorite. And your mother was a Hittite. On the day you were born, your cord was not cut. You were not washed with water for cleansing. You were not rubbed with salt. You were not wrapped in cloths. No one would do any of these things for you. No, you were thrown out into the open field. This is because you were hated on the day you were born. Then I passed by and saw you kicking about in your blood. I said to you, "Live!"'" (ICB).

**1 Corinthians 13:1** "I may speak in different languages of men or even angels. But if I do not have love, then I am only a noisy bell or a ringing cymbal" (ICB).

## Can We Smell Love?

Like the sweet fragrance of flowers,
Perfume savored for hours and hours,
Day or night, bundled warm in love's nest,
Never fearful of harm 'cause I know I am blest.

**Song of Solomon 1:3** "The smell of your perfume is pleasant. Your name is pleasant like expensive perfume! That's why the young women love you" (ICB).

**Can We Taste Love?**
No one really tastes love, like the mangoes on the tree;
But love is quite enjoyable, and important to me.
It's what you and I were made for, and happily I find
I have nurture in abundance, because it's God's design.

**Job 6:6-7** "Tasteless food is not eaten without salt. There is no flavor in the white part of an egg. I refuse to touch it. Such food makes me sick" (ICB).

Yes, even babes can recognize
love in their moms and in their dads,
For there is nothing that resides there,
that would make a kid feel bad.

**Psalm 103:13** "The Lord has mercy on those who fear him, as a father has mercy on his children" (ICB).

**Matthew 7:11** "Even though you are bad, you know how to give good gifts to your children. So surely your heavenly Father will give good things to those who ask him" (ICB).

Love usually looks like a broad smile,
or wide, welcoming arms.
Love feels like a big, strong hug,
that would shield from every harm.

**Mark 9:42** "If one of these little children believes in me, and someone causes that child to sin, then it will be very bad for him. It would be better for him to have a large stone tied around his neck and be drowned in the sea" (ICB).

Love sounds like a gentle and encouraging voice that is hardly ever loud. Love's scent is not frightful, and it makes us proud, not cowed.

**Colossians 4:6** "When you talk, you should always be kind and wise. Then you will be able to answer everyone in the way you should" (ICB).

Love is full of flavor, sometimes savory [*practical empathy*],
sometimes sweet [*caresses*],
But at other times, because of sin, bitter experiences
[*illness and stern discipline*] we meet.

**Hebrews 6:4-6** "Some people cannot be brought back again to a changed life. They were once in God's light. They enjoyed heaven's gift, and they shared in the Holy Spirit. They found out how good God's word is, and they received the powers of his new world. And then they fell away from Christ! It is not possible to keep on bringing them back to a changed life again. For they are nailing the Son of God to a cross again and are shaming him in front of others" (ICB).

Love's eyes are real discerning,
spotting dangers from afar.
But the things you need for thriving
are what they are truly looking for.

Love makes no excuses,
but rises with each challenging condition;
For the indomitable love,
there can be no failed mission.

**1 Corinthians 13:4-6** "Love is patient and kind. Love is not jealous, it does not brag, and it is not proud. Love is not rude, is not selfish, and does not become angry easily. Love does not remember wrongs done against it. Love takes no pleasure in evil, but rejoices over the truth" (ICB).

**2 Chronicles 16:9** "The Lord searches all the earth for people who have given themselves completely to him. He wants to make them strong" (ICB).

**1 John 4:18** "Where God's love is, there is no fear, because God's perfect love takes away fear. It is punishment that makes a person fear. So love is not made perfect in the person who has fear" (ICB).

We invite you to view the complete
selection of titles we publish at:
**www.TEACHServices.com**

We encourage you to write us
with your thoughts about this,
or any other book we publish at:
**info@TEACHServices.com**

TEACH Services' titles may be purchased in
bulk quantities for educational, fund-raising,
business, or promotional use.
**bulksales@TEACHServices.com**

Finally, if you are interested in seeing
your own book in print, please contact us at:
**publishing@TEACHServices.com**

We are happy to review your manuscript at no charge.

www.ingramcontent.com/pod-product-compliance
Lightning Source LLC
Chambersburg PA
CBHW061119170426
43200CB00023B/2998